Clouds

Rourke Educational Media
rourkeeducationalmedia.com

Precious McKenzie

Before & After Reading Activities

Teaching Focus:

Consonant Blends- Look in the book to find words that begin with a consonant blend such as st, sm, or pr.

Before Reading:

Building Academic Vocabulary and Background Knowledge

Before reading a book, it is important to set the stage for your child or student by using pre-reading strategies. This will help them develop their vocabulary, increase their reading comprehension, and make connections across the curriculum.

1. *Read the title and look at the cover. Let's make predictions about what this book will be about.*
2. *Take a picture walk by talking about the pictures/photographs in the book. Implant the vocabulary as you take the picture walk. Be sure to talk about the text features such as headings, Table of Contents, glossary, bolded words, captions, charts/ diagrams, or Index.*
3. Have students read the first page of text with you then have students read the remaining text.
4. *Strategy Talk – use to assist students while reading.*
   - *Get your mouth ready*
   - *Look at the picture*
   - *Think…does it make sense*
   - *Think…does it look right*
   - *Think…does it sound right*
   - *Chunk it – by looking for a part you know*
5. *Read it again.*

Content Area Vocabulary

Use glossary words in a sentence.

condense
droplets
hail
predict

After Reading:

Comprehension and Extension Activity

After reading the book, work on the following questions with your child or students in order to check their level of reading comprehension and content mastery.

1. *Describe the water cycle. (Summarize)*
2. *What happens when water on Earth evaporates? (Asking Questions)*
3. *What are clouds made of? (Asking Questions)*
4. *What type of clouds can you see in the sky right now? (Text to Self Connection)*

Extension Activity

In your classroom, create a chart. Label the days of the week. For each day, record the types of clouds you see in the sky. Write down what the weather was like on each day. Think about the types of clothing you should wear for the weather. How can you be prepared?

Table of Contents

Water Everywhere

What are clouds? Clouds are groups of water **droplets**.

How do water droplets get up to the sky? It's all part of the water cycle.

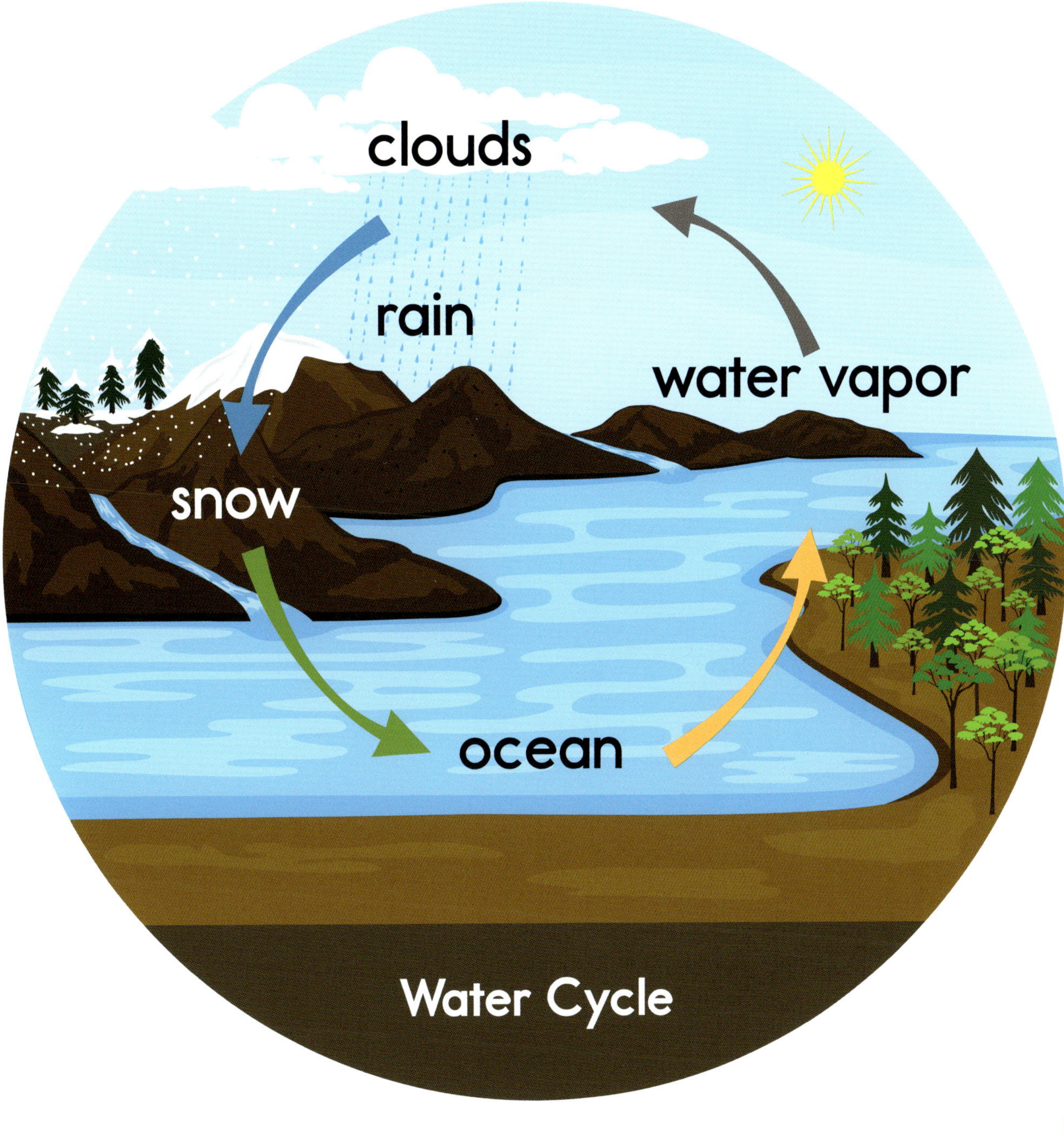
clouds
rain
water vapor
snow
ocean
Water Cycle

There's water all around us. It's in rivers, lakes, oceans, and puddles.

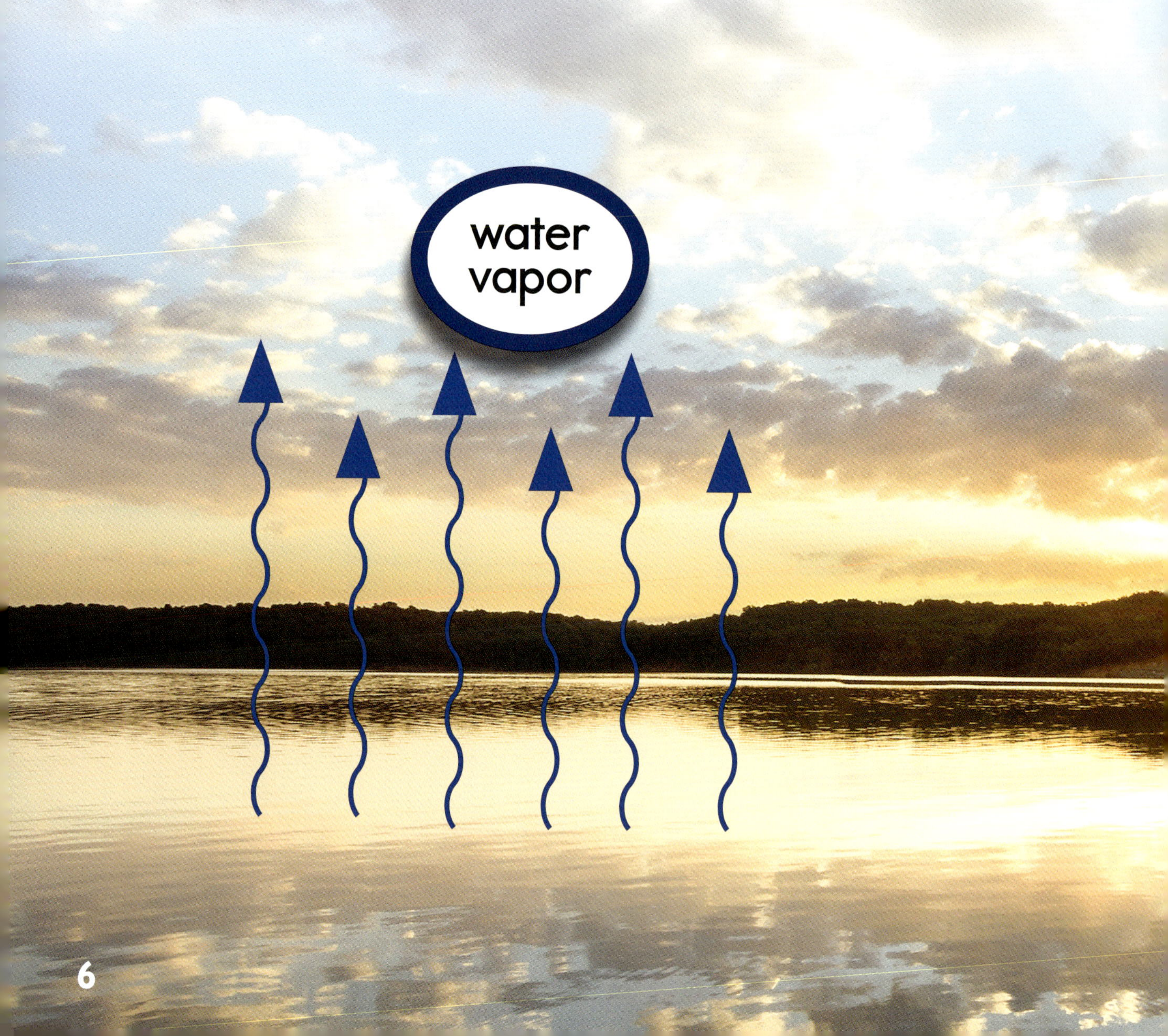

The sun heats some of the water. It turns from liquid into a gas. This is called water vapor. The vapor rises into the cool air.

The cool air makes the water vapor **condense**. This forms clouds.

The water droplets fall back down as rain, **hail**, ice, or snow. The water cycle continues again and again.

Weather Ahead!

The shape and color of clouds can tell you about the weather.

Cirrus clouds tell us it will be a nice, sunny day.

Cirrus clouds are high in the sky.
They are wispy and thin.

Stratus clouds are low and gray. They can produce rain or snow.

Stratocumulus clouds can be gray or white. They form in sheets or layers. They look like honeycombs.

Cumulus clouds are bright and puffy. They contain ice and water droplets. Cumulus clouds signal good weather.

Cumulonimbus clouds are tall, heavy, and stacked. They bring rough weather such as thunder, lightning, and hail. Cumulonimbus clouds can also bring tornadoes!

lightning

Clouds and You

Go outside. Look at the color, shape, and height of the clouds. What are they? What type of weather do they **predict**?

Cloud Facts

- A cloud can contain more than a million pounds (500,000 kilograms) of water.

- Cirrus clouds are sometimes called "mare's tails" because they are shaped like a horse's tail.

- Snow, sleet, rain, and hail falling from clouds is called precipitation.

- Water vapor weighs less than air. That's one reason clouds float high in the sky.

Picture Glossary

condense (kuhn-DENSS): When a gas or vapor condenses, it becomes a liquid because it has cooled.

droplets (DROP-lets): Droplets are very small particles of ice or water.

hail (HAYL): A small ball of ice that falls from the clouds.

predict (pri-DIKT): When someone predicts something, that means they say what they think will happen.

Index

Websites to Visit

http://easyscienceforkids.com/all-about-clouds
www.weatherforkids.org/clouds.html
https://kidskonnect.com/science/clouds

About the Author

Precious McKenzie lives in Montana. She loves being outdoors, visiting parks, and sharing Mother Nature with her three children and three dogs.

www.rourkeeducationalmedia.com

PHOTO CREDITS: Cover and title page: ©NithidPhoto/iStock; p.5: ©Meera Yellamaraju; p.6-7: ©tomofbluesprings; p.8-9, 23: ©Alex Potemkin; p.11: ©simonbradfield; p.12-13: ©sarahgerrity; p.14: ©Solodov Aleksey; p.15: ©Christopher PB, ©Volosina; p.17: ©ivanastar; p.18-19: ©Clint Spencer; p.21, 23: ©Chris Bernard; p.23: ©ultramarinfoto, ©David Parsons

Edited by: Keli Sipperley
Cover design by: Nicola Stratford www.nicolastratford.com
Interior design by: Rhea Magaro-Wallace

Library of Congress PCN Data

Clouds / Precious McKenzie
(Mother Nature)
ISBN (hard cover)(alk. paper) 978-1-68342-320-1
ISBN (soft cover) 978-1-68342-416-1
ISBN (e-Book) 978-1-68342-486-4
Library of Congress Control Number: 2017931168

Printed in the United States of America, North Mankato, Minnesota